Set Backs and Step Ups

Set Backs and Step Ups

Jeff Jarrell

Setbacks and Steps Up

Copyright ©2023 by Jeff Jarrell

All rights reserved.

Published in 2023.

Illustrations by Chloe Lineberg

Cover Design by Sean Paul Lavine

ISBN 979-8-218-22822-4 Paperback

Library of Congress Control Number: Available upon request.

Printed in the United States of America.

Clyde Custom Publishing

4207 SE Woodstock Blvd. #253

Portland, OR 97206

ClydeCustomPublishing.com

All proceed from your purchase of this book are donated to:

Community Autism Resources & Education Systems - CARES

Contents

Set Backs and Step Ups	9
Set Backs Don't Give Notice	13
Healing Takes Time	17
Steps Up Come in Many Forms	21
It Can Happen to Anyone	23
Love Stories	27
Becoming a Family	31
Welcome to America!	33
The 9 to 5 of Life	37
Building From The Ground Up	41
On My Own	45
Established and Still Learning	47
Breaking a Sweat	49
When It Pains, It Pours	51
All In For Family	53
Every Child is Different	44
Even Though It Hurts	57
Our Paths are Paved With Steps	59
Thank You	61

Set Backs and Step Ups

Today

Just get up.

If I have said that to myself once, I've said it hundreds of times.

Just get up, Jeff. Move forward.

Life changes in the blink of an eye. It can be great. It can be lousy. And when it knocks you down, you land hard. I know it. You know it. And if there's one thing I've learned in the past 20 years, it is this: The longer you wallow, the harder it gets to step up and get going.

I believe all of us have set backs. None of us know for sure how we will react when a big one knocks us down. Yet I have discovered in myself and others close to me the will people have to get back up. We take it one step at a time. We look for *and* see the good. We reach within for the best we can give and are willing to open the proverbial door of opportunity. And we always must remember when that door opens, we are the ones who decide to go through it and take a new path. We have to step up.

Set Backs Don't Give Notice

Oct 1984

It was foggy at 11:30 p.m. on Friday night, October 19, 1984. I was headed home after a party in Charleston. Driving my red Ford Escort, I just reached the intersection of Greenbrier Street and Airport Road when a car came speeding toward me. At the time, there was no guardrail at the intersection. I made a hard left. My car flew across two lanes and into a ditch. My head hit the windshield. I was in shock and had a concussion. Although I cannot remember what I was thinking, I made an unconscious decision that forever changed my life. I decided to crawl up on the road.

Occasionally, I have a flashback about that night. I am crawling in the dark when I see a bright light coming toward me. The light consumes me. Then, everything goes black.

On that night, I crawled out of the ditch and crossed two lanes of Greenbrier Street. I kept crawling up the hill to Charleston.

A man driving a pick-up truck saw a dark crumpled pile on the road. In the dark, foggy night, he thought it was a trash bag. He drove right over it. He dragged me under the truck for about 40 yards until his girlfriend heard me scream. She shouted at him to stop.

Screaming in pain as I was dragged along the asphalt, my body took a horrendous beating. My left hip was dislocated. My right leg was crushed. My right ear was hanging loosely from my head. I had a serious cut around my right eye. My back looked like ground meat.

The rescue team found me wedged behind the right rear axle. They had to lift the truck to get me out.

I never met the couple in the pick-up truck and don't know who they are. I can't imagine what the driver went through when he realized it was a person, not trash, he hit that night. I cast no blame, he couldn't have known. I imagine he was almost as grateful as I am his girlfriend heard me cry out. I'd love to meet him. I'd like to tell him I am okay. I'd like to tell him he changed my life – for the better. I learned to get up.

"As a mother, answering the phone late at night is always an iffy thing when you know one of your children is out," says Barbara Jarrell. "Answering a call from the State Police is a nightmare. When the trooper called our house that night and told me Jeff had been in an accident and transported to Charleston General Hospital, I was shocked and petrified. I couldn't even process what they were telling. I couldn't fathom the pain he was in."

It is terrifying to sit and wait, not knowing whether your child will live or die. It doesn't matter how old they are or what happened. For a mother, all you can think about is he is my child, he is terribly injured, how can I stop the pain. To this day, remembering that night and the weeks following bring all of the fear and pain right back like it was yesterday.

I woke up 72 hours later on Monday afternoon. I was in Charleston General Hospital. I didn't know what happened but I knew it wasn't good.

Miraculously, I had no internal injuries; physically I was a mess. My left eye was swollen. My ear was bandaged and I could see the scrapes on my face, arms and legs. I could not see the damage to my back. My left leg was in traction. My right leg was splinted to allow the bones to grow back. Because of the serious nature of the breaks in my right leg, Dr. William Sale, my orthopedic surgeon, used a Hoffman's devise to keep the bones in place. That devise is a pin not unlike the meat pick in your mother's holiday nutcracker set. It screws through the bone and is held in place with bands that are tightened or moved as the leg mends.

"Seeing him in that hospital bed with those injuries was a nightmare. As I sat there that weekend, I worried There was so much wrong with him and I wondered how he would make it and how he would be. My husband and I prayed for strength for all of us. Jeff was going to have to work through this pain and more to heal.

I was in the hospital for almost six weeks. During that time of healing and therapy, I discovered how hard it is to step up physically and emotionally. The pain could be indescribable at times.

When I think back, I remember light moments in those dark days.

I was blessed with good surgeons. Dr. William Sale was my orthopedic surgeon; Dr. Alfonso Amores was my plastic surgeon. While Dr. Sale mended my bones, Dr. Amores performed plastic surgery on my right leg, left hand, severed ear and the cut over my eye. They patched the ragged and torn skin on my back. Dr. Amores is a true artist in his profession and I am a living example of his handiwork. My parents teased Dr. Sale that he "signed" his exceptional work. The surgical scar on my left butt cheek is shaped like an "S".

The physicians pulled no punches. My injuries were serious and my healing process was not a one-and-done surgery. There were multiple surgeries. There were skin grafts. There were pins. There was pain. At one point, I asked the doctor why it hurt so much when I coughed or laughed. Half-joking, he told me I probably had a couple of broken ribs but there were so many more serious injuries, they hadn't checked for them. He assured me the ribs would heal.

I lay in the hospital bed the first few days and wondered how I would get on. Looking at my seriously damaged legs, I faced some big questions. Would I be able to walk again? Drive again? Run again? Running was my life.

Somehow, lying there, I realized what I had to do. I had to get up.

Healing Takes Time

Oct - Nov 1984

The hard road of physical therapy did not make it easier to answer my questions. On my first day of physical therapy, the physical therapists placed me on a special board. They moved the board to a 45 degree angle. It was excruciating. Then they moved it to 90 degrees. The pain was unimaginable. We were done for the day.

I remember when two therapists placed me on a low bed and put a skate on my left leg. They wanted to see if I could move my leg like a windshield wiper. I couldn't. . **Step up, Jeff.**

Those weeks were tough. Finally, one day they got me up on the parallel bars and asked me to see if I could take a step. It took three therapists to get me upright on the bars. When I stood up, I got instantly dizzy but I got about half a step in.

When my mother got to the hospital, I was so excited. I said, "Mom! I can walk! I can walk again!" Little did I know how much more therapy I would face. That one small step was huge for me. But it didn't mean I'd be running any time soon. Not even walking came without more work and lots of pain.

Nick and I had two children at home who couldn't drive and we worked full-time jobs, so we could not be with Jeff all day. My mother came to help us at home. I would go to the hospital every day after work and we would be there on weekends. Seeing him make progress, even in small ways, was a blessing. But there was so much to do, it was hard for Jeff to think he'd get over it all and be okay again.

The accident and aftermath changed Jeff. He became more humble and more caring. He was facing the hardest moment of his life and he knew it. I believe he knew it was hard for us, too.

I sometimes think back to that time and realize even through the pain of recovery, I have no memory of thinking, "Why me?" I have no memory of being angry or resentful, although I am certain I had those moments. When I ask my mother about that time of recovery, she says we took everything one step at a time and focused on each step toward recovery. **Get up, Jeff.**

At first, when I was in the hospital, I knew what happened to me. I heard all the medical explanations and felt the pain. But, because I could not remember the accident, I didn't have the visual understanding. On Monday, November 18, I got the picture.

Watching Monday Night football with thousands of other fans, I saw Joe Thiemann sacked by New York Giants linebackers Lawrence Taylor and Harry Carson. Along with the players on the field, fans in the stadium and television viewers I saw him suffer a compound fracture of the tibia and fibula in his right leg.

I saw the players gather around him and call for help. I saw the team medics come running. I saw the replays. I knew his pain. I knew his fate. I had the same injury. I almost threw up. I immediately called my parents and asked them if they were watching the game.

　I was blessed with my parents, especially my mother, who was at the hospital as much as she could be. Their steadfast and unwavering support as I made slow progress was important for me. And their faith that God would give me strength was every bit as important.

I also was blessed to have as a roommate the son of my junior high school history teacher, Alma Berry. Her son had been admitted to the hospital for severe diabetes. He was fighting for his life in a different way than I was, but we were both fighting just the same. His mother's positive attitude and focus was good for both of us.

At Spring Hill Junior High School, blue-haired Ms. Berry was a favorite of most students in the school. She knew just what it took to get each of her students in line when we needed a nudge. She was not shy about making her thoughts clear. I will never forget the day she took me aside in class and said, "Jefferson, get it together, brotha!" She knew what her students were capable of and she expected them to live up to those abilities.

At the hospital, she reminded me I would be the one responsible for getting back to a healthy life. She said, "Learn your terms and set goals for meet them." **Step up, Jeff. Move forward.**

Steps Up Come in Many Forms

1985 - 1986

You have to take one step at a time.

Once I was out of the hospital, I continued therapy. Much of that, like the therapy I had in the hospital, is blurry. Physical recovery is hard and painful. Emotionally and mentally, the recovery isn't any easier. Up to that point in my life, I thought I was invincible. I found out the hard way that was not so.

I desperately wanted to get back to school. I realized I needed to set a course for my life, following Ms. Berry's admonition that I get it together.

West Virginia State College administration and faculty could not have been more supportive. The school made accommodations for me to get in and out of classes because I was walking on crutches when I first returned to college. Generously, the WVSC athletic department gave me a letterman's sweater for my time on the track team.

Again, my mom was number one on my team. With everything else she was doing, she added chauffer to her schedule. She drove me to school and picked me up. She took me to therapy and doctors' appointments. She took me wherever I needed to go. She was my cheerleader.

My mother was a great help after Jeff came home. She stayed with him during the day and helped change his bandages. He was learning so much all over again. Walking was the big thing, but it wouldn't be the only thing he had to figure out. That first day I dropped him off at State was like the first day I left him at grade school. I was as nervous about how he would do as I was when he was six years old.

Academically, I turned it on. I always had an interest in statistics and was enamored of the stock market. I worked as a temporary employee at Columbia Gas Transmission's corporate office in Charleston, going to work each day with my parents.

Getting back to school helped me get my confidence back. It helped me see a different life perspective that included a career. It was visible and physical proof I could overcome a major setback.

Some steps were harder than I thought they would be. One of those was getting into a car and driving. At the time, we lived by Little Creek Park in Spring Hill. I remember how nervous my mother and I were the first time I got behind the wheel of a car after the accident. I drove a short distance to Little Creek Park and back. By myself. **I stepped up.**

Another important step up for me was getting involved in something that wasn't about me.

My best friend, Kevin, coached girls' volleyball at Calvary Baptist Church in Nitro where his father was the pastor. He asked me to coach with him. Because I always loved sports and have a competitive nature, I took him up on the offer.

It might be curious to think about coaching youth sports as transformative. For me, it was huge. Coaching challenged me to see a broader perspective on life. Coaching the girls gave me a sense of purpose that was more than just about me. I found a new sense of community in volunteering for the team. I am sure they don't know it, but the girls on that team did more for me than I ever did for them.

I was raised in a Christian family. My parents were, and are, good examples of living a life that is built on honesty, belief in God and service to family and community. Over the months of my recovery, those concepts became important practices to me. They became a part of who I was then and who I am now. I found real value in prayer and giving to others. They are guideposts and actions.

Each step of my recovery had an impact on me. I found my heart had changed completely. My faith in God became stronger. I accepted Jesus as my Savior. My life was changing. I realized how important it is to look up and be positive. **I was stepping up.**

Step up, Jeff.

It Can Happen to Anyone

1986 - 1987

The money is gone. You can't get it back. Following the accident, I received a $50,000 settlement from our insurance company. I paid medical bills with some of it. I spent some to send my parents on a trip to the Bahamas. After all they had and were doing for me, I wanted to show them how much I appreciated them.

In 1986, I invested the remaining $40,000 with Doug Squire, a family friend who owned an investment company. His correspondence always came on fancy letterhead and he told me he was setting my account up with limited stock offerings at the best rates and terms. When the limited stock offerings terms came up, Doug would say he had another deal to roll the money into and keep making money for me. I had no reason to question his advice.

A few times I ask Doug for some of my money. Once I asked him for $3,000. He said he would just give me the money and take care of the paperwork later. After a while, he began delaying and delaying payments and I lost touch with him.

Afraid of what might be happening, I talked to an attorney. After investigating, the attorney told me that Doug was involved in racketeering in a Ponzi scheme. That is an investment fraud in which existing investors are paid with funds from new investors. What Doug would do when I asked for money was find a new investor and take that person's money and give it to me.

My money was gone. I lost my savings to a schemer who not only bilked me but a substantial number of other people in the Kanawha Valley.

In the "What Did You Learn from This?" lesson book, I learned a few important things. I learned to trust people who proved themselves to be reliable and invested in serving their clients honestly and legally. I learned to be honest with people and upfront in my dealings with others. I learned to put what I knew about how to treat people into practice, not just sometimes, but every time, no matter what the circumstances.

I stepped up and put more emphasis on doing unto others as I would have them do unto me.

Love Stories

1991 - 1992... and Forever ♡

Love me, love me not. True love isn't always first love.

In my early 20s, I married a young woman I knew for a short time. At first, we were fine. Then our relationship became rocky. We grew apart before we had time to really grow together. We were married for four years. One day, she went to visit her parents and never came back.

I can't say for sure what happened. I have a few theories. My first wife adored her father who was a good man and a protector. Perhaps it is true that you can't replace a girl's father. Also, she was in a serious relationship before we met. Perhaps she realized she made a mistake leaving that relationship for ours.

I had to acknowledge what a setback a failed marriage could be. I had to work through the sadness, the disappointment and the facts. I learned sometimes you just can't match up to an important person in another person's life. I learned not to take people and their feelings at face value; we all have emotional baggage. I learned sometimes what's deep in our hearts and minds isn't easy to discover, to express or to attain. **Step up, Jeff.**

Then, I found my soul mate via telephone, a facsimile machine ... and a dog!

Joyce and I met in 1991 when worked for insurance companies. I was in Charleston; she was in Columbus, Ohio. We talked on the phone a few times a week about business and not too much small talk. We had a typical workplace relationship.

I knew she liked dogs so when I got a dachshund puppy I named Hogan, I told her about him. She asked if I'd send her a picture. She never sent it back. In fact, she still has it.

I thought it was odd she'd keep a picture of my dog, so I mentioned it to her one day in January 1993. I casually suggested she could bring it back herself if she came to Charleston. To my surprise, she took me up on the invitation!

As Joyce recalls: *Jeff and I worked together – via phone and fax. He seemed nice and genuine. When I asked him to send me a photo of his new dog, he did! Then he invited me to bring it back myself, I decided to take the chance and didn't have any serious expectations about the visit. Plus, I really wanted to meet Hogan!*

I stepped up for this date! I bought flowers, I planned to make dinner. Joyce would get to know me and Hogan. It was less and less about the return of the picture and more about meeting a new person.

At 3 p.m. on the Friday afternoon she was coming, she called me from Parkersburg. Her car broke down on her way from Columbus. It was my chance to be a knight in shining armor! If ever there was a time when I knew I needed to step up, this was it! **Step up, Jeff.**

I called a friend in Parkersburg who said he could take care of getting her car repaired and ready for her to pick up on Sunday. When I got to Parkersburg, I could see her on the pay phone at the restaurant where she was waiting for me. She was beautiful. I remember looking at her and, right out loud, saying "Wow!" I think I double-stepped up when I met Joyce.

Except for Hogan throwing up on Joyce, the weekend was great. I grilled chicken and vegetables for dinner. At the time, it might have been the only thing I really knew how to cook. My family came over to meet her.

She came back for Valentine's Day and we went to the Reba McIntire concert in Charleston. We were talking on the phone every day and getting together on weekends. By Memorial Day, we were engaged. In October, we were married.

While Joyce and I were head over heels in love, there were quite a few naysayers among my families and friends. Kevin told me to slow down; this was just a rebound and couldn't last.

I can't pinpoint a certain thing that made me feel like our relationship was right; I just knew we were in love. My friends and family didn't share any concerns about our relationship if they had them. They just told me to be careful.

Also, I knew from the start Jeff had a strong faith and it was, and is, one of the things that I love about him. To this day, we share a strong faith. It's important in both of our lives.

The move to Charleston from Columbus was a leap of faith for Joyce. It meant such big changes in her life. A native of Pittsburgh, PA, she was used to big city life. In Columbus, she was up for a substantial raise if she stayed. Moving to Charleston meant she would sacrifice her career.

Yet, she came. We lived first in Rock Lake Village and later moved to Teays Valley. Joyce found a job she enjoyed at Smart Temporary Services and then moved to Animal Care Associates. Later, when we moved to Winfield, she began working as a preschool teacher's aide at Winfield United Methodist Church. Eventually, the preschool director retired and the church asked Joyce to take the position.

You learn from every life experience. Being open to finding love has made all the difference for Joyce and me. We both stepped up

Becoming a Family

1999 - 2005

When one door closes, another – maybe even three – opens.

There was, however, one thing: I wanted to be a father. While having a family was not as important to Joyce, she understood how I felt.

Having our own children was not in the cards for us. We went through every test there was, some excruciatingly embarrassing and stressful. We talked about our choices. We faced the harsh and disappointing reality that having our own children was not in God's plan. We wondered if this meant God did not want us to have children at all.

The setback was hard to face. We decided to look into adoption. I will always be grateful that we did. I am a dad. Joyce is the best mother in the world!

I was 33 when Jeff and I got married and didn't start any family planning right away. Due to my age, I wasn't surprised at the difficulty I was having with pregnancy issues. However, adoption was always something I thought about and I was willing to go through the process knowing we could give a baby or a child a new opportunity and share in building our family.

Adoption is not for the weak of spirit. In our case, each of our three children's arrivals were blessed adventures. **Joyce and I step up for our family.**

In 1999, Joyce and I attended a workshop about international adoptions sponsored by St. John's United Methodist Church.

We met a team from Burlington United Methodist Ministries that was helping with adoptions from Korea. We went through pre-adoption testing. We took a home study survey that asked difficult and probing questions about us and all aspects of our lives. We had to go to Bethesda, Maryland, for in-person interviews. We learned that, if a child came available that was a match for us, we would have to pay for an escort to bring the baby from Korea to the United States.

We waited and we prayed. We weren't sure when – or if – the adoption agency would find a match. In late 1999, we learned we would get a four-month old baby boy! Noah Davis Hyo Jarrell would arrive at Dulles Airport outside of Washington DC from Korea on July 4, 2000. We could pick him up there. Joyce, my mother and I drove to Washington to meet him. We had an anxious hour waiting at the airport for the escort to arrive with our baby boy. He cried inconsolably the entire way from Washington to Teays Valley. We were so worried and stressed. I'm glad my mother was there to help us. We named our baby Noah. He was home for the Fourth of July!

A little more than a year later, we decided to grow our family. This time, we worked with an adoption placement service in Michigan. Naomi SaRang Jarrell was nine months old when she arrived in October 2002 at the Columbus, Ohio, airport. Her arrival was a little more of an adventure than Noah's was. Joyce, my mother, my sister, Noah and I traveled to Columbus to pick her up. We stayed the night in a hotel and planned to drive home after we picked her up the next day. Naomi left Korea and traveled with an escort to Los Angeles then Columbus. At the airport, the escort came through the terminal wheeling Naomi in a small stroller. She walked up to us and asked, "Are you Jarrell?" We said yes. She handed the stroller to us and said. "Good Luck! She's a good baby. I have to go and catch my next plane." She was off and we were standing there with a new baby girl in an adorable pink outfit. We had our girl!

In 2005, Joyce decided she wanted one more child. I was on board!

On a Friday afternoon while Noah and Naomi were napping, Joyce sat down at her computer and visited a website called Rainbow Kids. There she found Lily Vilma Jarrell and knew she was the one for us. Born in Guatemala, she was about 2 and ½ years old and ready for a family. Joyce immediately followed up with the Children's Home Society in Medina, Ohio. Trouble was, the adoption process was a first-come, first-served system and another family was interested in Lily, too.

Joyce called me told me where we stood. With little time to spare, we needed to get papers signed, complete forms and send in a deposit. The first family that completed that work would have Lily. Poor Joyce! She couldn't stand the stress of getting the papers in order. She turned the adoption business and communications over to me and headed for Walmart!

I freaked out. It was exciting to think we could have another child and yet unnerving to realize I had a short time to get everything done. I accomplished the task in record time; when Joyce got home, I was able to say, "We got our girl!"

Noah, Naomi and Lily are the names that we gave our children. When they came to us, each had a given name from their homelands. Respecting that, and wanting to be sure they knew they had special stories, we kept their given names for their middle names.

Persistence paid off! I stepped up. Little did I know I'd be stepping up again to bring our girl home.

Welcome to America!

2000

The agency said we had two choices for Lily's arrival. We could wait for them to find an escort or we could come to Guatemala to pick her up. The agency was not sure when an escort could be arranged.

On Monday, I traveled to Guatemala to pick Lily up. Joyce stayed home with Noah and Naomi. We were so excited we paid little attention to weather reports that Hurricane Rita was picking up steam in the Gulf Coast.

My plan was to leave Guatemala on Thursday. Armed with our new daughter, adoption and travel papers, diapers, sippy cup, rattles and books, I left Guatemala and headed to the United States. We moved quickly through customs at the Houston airport. Our next step was to catch a plane for Charleston.

Everything was cool – until we got to the main terminal where I learned Hurricane Rita was headed our way. The city of Houston and the airport were under mandatory orders to evacuate everyone and the airport was closing as Lily and I were standing at the loading gate for our flight. **Step up, Jeff!**

Two men who worked for Kanawha Scales in Poca were also scheduled for that flight. Quickly, I reached out to Raymond Crockett, our travel agent, and they reached out to theirs. Raymond really stepped up! He found a flight headed to Washington, D.C.'s Reagan Airport and arranged for tickets and a hotel room in D.C. Lily and I arrived in Washington late in the evening after a long, stressful day. On the shuttle from the airport to the hotel, two elderly women could sense my stress. They were compassionate when they heard our story.

At the hotel, I learned the hotel general manager knew how to step up, too. Raymond had explained my situation to him. He went out of his way to make us comfortable even for our short stay. When Lily and I arrived at the hotel, we found toiletries, diapers, milk, and baby items waiting for us in our room

When we arrived home, family and friends were there to greet us. I was exhausted and needed a nap. Lily, on the other hand, was having the time of her life, taking a bubble bath in a bucket.

Of course, I expected that adoption would change our lives. I wasn't sure what those changes would look like, but I have faith and we worked through the obstacles together, just as we have done with everything that's come our way in our lives.

We have so many opportunities in life to step up if only we recognize them and realize what they can mean for someone. . **Strangers with good hearts stepped up!**

The 9 to 5 of Life

1988

You're fired!

The shock that registers with you when you hear those words is unforgettable, especially if it comes as a complete surprise. It is, at first, unimaginable. Then, once the stun – and sting – wear off, it is frightening. I know. It happened to me.

Right out of college, I landed a job with a Charleston company in January 1988. I was hired as a sales trainee. After six months in training, I was offered two transfer choices. The first was to an office in Bakersfield, California; the second opportunity was in Trenton, New Jersey. The jobs were both at the same $15,000 annual salary I was making here in West Virginia and $500 for moving expenses. I did not think I could afford the price of living in those areas on that salary. I turned them both down.

After I turned the second offer down, my supervisor asked me to meet with the Personnel Office. There, I was told to clean out my desk and leave the building. I lost my job by saying no for the second time.

In retrospect, I realize I did not understand the opportunity to move to another location was not an option; it was part of the sales trainee system. I thought after training I would be assigned to the local warehouse or one of the company departments in the main office. What *was* an option was to elect which city I wanted to go to and not whether I wanted to go at all.

I was deflated and angry. I felt like the company let me down. I never expected this outcome. I was so confident I was doing a good job and then this!

I needed to get my act together. I couldn't let this slow me down! I took a sales job that paid me on commission. It was a start but it was terrible.

Looking back, I think my early professional fits and starts were all in God's plan. What happened, happened. I am not bitter when setbacks happen; I think that helps me move forward. In fact, I believe just like setbacks blindside you, steps up come in surprising ways and propel you forward.

Thinking about my next steps led me to recall how much I like working with people. When I was in high school, I participated in two programs that gave me the best preparation I could have ever had for my life's work. They are Junior Achievement and Dale Carnegie.

In Junior Achievement, I learned how to select a product, make the product and sell the product. I learned how to make a business plan and carry it out. I learned the importance of knowing my product so I could sell it and the importance of good client relations. I was fortunate to be on a team selected to make a presentation at the National Junior Achievement Conference. I was even more fortunate to be the presenter.

From Dale Carnegie, I learned presentation is important and relating to the people with whom you are speaking is equally as important. Whether it's a one-on-one conversation or a presentation before a large group of people, you need to know your audience as well as your subject. You need to know how to read their reactions and make adjustments to your conversations and presentations.

From both of these programs, I learned I like finance and business and I like working with people. I learned I could be good at it.

Throughout my life, regardless of the situation, I find the key to moving forward is being a good, active listener. It is as important to listen, and really hear, what people are saying as it is to be sure they hear you. It also is important to make sure you are listening so you understand them.

Setbacks can blindside you. You don't always, if ever, see them coming. Step up, Jeff!

Building From The Ground Up

1989

I talked to my parents about my work situation and they suggested I talk to Larry Kaltnecker, a family friend who owned an insurance business. Larry told me about the diverse options for insurance companies. I could sell home and auto insurance, which everyone is familiar with, and I could also sell life and health insurance. I just needed to get a license. So I did a three month self-study course and set out to get a job.

Larry recommended I call on Chuck Austin because he knew Chuck's business was growing and thought he might be looking for someone to join him. With my license in hand, I confidently headed to Chuck's company office to put in my resume and go to work.

I left my resume because Chuck was out of the office. It seemed he was always out of the office. Determined to get to work, I went to his office one day and waited for him to return from lunch. When he got back to the office, one of the women in the front office told him that I had been sitting there waiting to see him. He recognized my family name and invited me to come up to talk with him. He told me being an insurance agent was not a desk job. If I wanted to make a go at it, I had to be a go-getter. I would need to get out and meet people. Listen to what they needed. Help them meet their goals and stay with them.

That was April 1989. I got into insurance and never looked back. It was – and is – a good thing I'm an optimist because I've had a few setbacks on the road to business success. **Stepping up made the difference!**

I know how fortunate I am to have had the opportunity to work for Chuck. We became great friends as well as good business partners. He taught me how to run a business. From him I learned more than the financial aspects of business ownership; I learned how to treat employees, vendors and clients. In 1989, I had the opportunity to start a life and health insurance department for the business. Starting from the ground up was a great way to understand the mechanics and the intricacies of running this business.

I loved it from the start!

I was doing it all on my own. I'd meet with potential clients in the evenings and get to know what they needed. I liked these kitchen table meetings when I could get to know my clients at home and really get a feel for what they needed. I could share ideas about what insurances might be best for them and match the plans to their budgets and their dreams for their futures.

I did the paperwork; I faxed and typed and copied and delivered. I was successful because I had listened to Chuck. I chose to be a go-getter. Get up, get dressed, show up. Go see people. **Step up!**

During my career, I have often thought about how sales parallels life. In sales, just like in life, you have to be present and make an effort to see positive results. You can let hearing no and having doors closed in your face bring you down OR you can keep going, realizing that the more doors that close, the closer you'll be to one that opens and someone says yes. You learn something every time you make a call. You have to learn to put it to use. You have to always look forward to the door that opens. **Stepping up when you have a setback keeps you on track.**

In my life, I have known many wonderful people. Chuck is one of the best. He treated me like a son. He took me under his wing and taught me the ropes of insurance. Working with him,

I learned what it meant to be a business owners and how to work with employees. I learned *it was not always easy, but it is rewarding.*

When I think back on my earliest experiences, I think of the people who took a chance with a young salesman and trusted me to do the right thing. I am amazed at how, when you do right by people, your own life can be enhanced.

One of the first people Chuck sent me to see was a local entrepreneur. I met with him and his wife and their son-in-law, who also worked in the business.

They became some of my first customers when they purchased life insurance from me. Over the years, as their family grew, they purchased life insurance for their children and their children's children. For 34 years, I have watched the family grow, I am proud to serve four generations of this family.

I am not just Mr. Jarrell, the insurance guy, I am Jeff. As the years have gone by, I have become part of the fabric of their family. They are more than commissions on the ledger for me. They are people who trust me. They rely on me. They believe that I will always step up for them. And because I value that relationship, I always will.

Chuck told me once, "When you are ready, I'll sell you this business. Just tell me when you're ready, Jeff."

In the spring of 1999, I decided I was ready. Over the past months, I had been keeping careful track of the sales for my unit. On paper, for the first time, I realized that the revenue from our work was up, but my income was not.

It was decision time for me. Joyce and I talked about the options. I told her I thought it was time for me to take the business on. She agreed with me and I went to talk to Chuck.

I had learned how to step up for clients and I knew I could step up for my own business. Step up, Jeff!

On My Own

1999

We had a great meeting. He offered to let me purchase the business from him for a purchase price plus 50 percent of the revenues for the first three years of my ownership or talk to a bank about a loan. I chose to take out a loan from One Valley Bank and I took over the business. One of the first moves I made was literal. I moved the offices from Spring Hill to Teays Valley, where our family lives.

My new business, The Jarrell Group, included life and health insurance and employee benefits. When I decided to purchase the business, I let all the clients I worked with know. Most of them stayed with me. I am most proud to say many of them are still with me, 34 years later. It says a lot for how I operate the business.

One of my long-time clients was a single mother of three boys when I met her. A bookkeeper for a Putnam County realtor and developer, she was looking for insurance when I went to her home one evening to talk with her.

When I arrived, she was making dinner and I went into the living room to hang out with one of her sons. In the living room, a chess game was set up. I introduced myself as Mr. Jeff and asked him if he wanted to play chess. He didn't know how, so I taught him while his mother made dinner. His mother is still one of my clients and so is that son. That was 28 years ago. The boy grew up, moved and away and recently returned to the area with his young family. He has a son who is ready to play chess now. I hope that Mr. Jeff, as I am still known in that family, gets a chance to teach that little boy, too.

My first hire was Becky. She was excited about joining my team. She was licensed and experienced. I did sales and we teamed up to do service. We grew the business and even added a part-time employee. Unfortunately, our partnership did not last. Becky was also my first fire. My first taste of management was bittersweet. It was a lesson in what could come.

During that time, I took on a new agent who eventually became my partner. We worked well together. I realized having a good business partner is similar to having a good marriage or personal relationship. You have to communicate and recognize you'll have ups and downs as you build your business. In a good business, just like in a good marriage, you work things out. Sometimes you have to regroup. You have to step up to move forward.

Like any industry, the insurance industry has its ups and its downs. The economy, business decisions and changing times have an effect on success and on business decisions. The company with whom I was working in my early insurance years decided to make some changes to their business. Those changes would not have been helpful to my business or my clients business. I was worried and afraid of a setback. I had clients, employees and my growing family to consider. I needed to make another big life decision. **I needed to step up to stay up.**

At the same time, I was facing hip replacement surgery. Like the insurance switch, it was not an optional thing and had to be done as well. From my hospital bed at Cabell Huntington Hospital, I called my contact at the insurance company and told him I was no longer going to sell its insurance. Fortunately, he understood my situation and made sure the company paid my medical bills and helped me make a smooth transition to a new company.

I am grateful to Scott Rider, one of my best friends to this day, because he suggested it might be time for me to switch companies and suggested the company I am with. The stress of doing this was overwhelming but I knew I had to do it. And I knew I had to do it right away.

Over the years, Scott has taught me – and reminded me more than once – that it is important to step up in all situations. Step up, Jeff!

Established and Still Learning

2013 - 2014

You took what?

Seven years into our partnership, I discovered that my partner stole from me. By working out a contract outside our company framework, he made commissions on new insurance policies that should have rightfully been done through the company. The first time it happened and I confronted him, he said he hadn't thought about it as stealing but he understood what I was saying. Yes, he understood. Then he did it again. This time when we talked about it, he said he did it and he'd do it again. True to his word, he did it a third time.

I was also in partnership with Michael Black. We shared office space and staff. When I left the partnership and office I had with my other partner, Michael left as well. After a few months, we decided to work together. This time, I was wiser and we agreed to go through the correct legal processes of registering the business and completing a formal agreement.

After a time, we outgrew this arrangement. Because we had a formal agreement in place, we knew how to work this out. We went through all of our accounts and made decisions about who would retain which clients.

Joyce was, as always, aware of my business activities and there to keep me on track. "Are you sure you know what you are doing?" she asked me when I told her about the plan to have a new business named JarrellBlack & Company. I was confident it was the right move. I decided to concentrate primarily on home and auto insurance, workers compensation insurance and some investments. My business plan was to put small business owners first and make their needs the priority of my business. After all, as a small business owner myself, I know the ups and downs of managing and planning and change.

Stand up for your principles. Doing the right thing is never wrong. Step up, Jeff!

Breaking a Sweat

2019 - 2020

I love a good workout. Always have. Always will.

I ran track before my car accident and got back into running and exercising as soon as I could during my recovery. Over the last 30 years or so I've kept up the running and participated in some charity and community running events.

I like cycling. Again, as with running, I'm all in. I enjoy a leisurely bike ride and I enjoy a competitive distance ride.

I like working out. Nothing does my body good like a cross training workout. In fact, I like it so much that in 2017 I became a certified CrossFit teacher and coach. The workouts are challenging and the instructors are encouraging. I like the workouts and I like the sense of community that I have built with others in the gym. I helped found the Teays Valley CrossFit and worked out there four to five days a week.

If you're an exercise fanatic, you know that some days are good and some not so good. I've had my share of pulled muscles and aching joints. Generally, I toughed them out. Slowing down when I needed to and being careful as I got back up to speed.

In December 2019, I went for my annual physical. For several months before that, I had some real trouble with body aches from my waist down. I was having a hard time getting out of bed. The doctor recommended I have blood work done.

In January 2020, the results came back. My thyroid was out of whack in a big way and I was beginning to suffer from rheumatoid arthritis. This was not good. I needed to see a specialist but could not get an appointment until May 2020.

Exercising as vigorously as I had been doing was out of the question. When a big part of your lifestyle changes, you have to make adjustments

By June, I was feeling even worse physically. On my right side, I was feeling pain and numbness from my waist down through my leg. But I am no quitter and a little pain was not going to stop me from doing what exercise I could. I tried deep tissue massage and visited a chiropractor. I had two steroid shots. Nothing helped appreciably.

Step up and get it figured out, Jeff!

When It Pains, It Pours

2020 - Today

Do you want the bad news or the bad news?

In talking with a friend who is a neurologist, I took a real psychological blow. He said he thought my problem could be one of two things and neither was good.

I couldn't stop my life.

It was August 2020, Joyce and I were driving Naomi to college in Tallahassee. In the hot Florida weather, I had a hard time breathing and experienced chest pains when we were moving our daughter into her dorm. I panicked and called my doctor. He told me to come into his office as soon as I got home. No appointment needed; he'd see me as soon as I got there.

If I thought I'd been tested enough for my aches and pains, I had another thing coming. The floodgates of medical research opened and pulled me in.

In September, I checked in to St. Mary's Hospital in Huntington for a heart cauterization which found no heart issues. However, an MRI I had about the same time showed a serious problem – a herniated disc in my spine.

The physician told Joyce and I my heart was fine but back surgery had to be done immediately. He explained I had been living with so much unrealized pain and it affected my whole body as I unconsciously compensated for it. In November, I had back surgery.

The surgery freed me from much of the pain. After several weeks off work, I headed back to the office.

Despite being vaccinated, I contracted COVID-19.

In October 2021, I was having serious problems with numbness in my hands and feet. My fingers and toes turned blue and then white when exposed to cold or when I was stressed. I was afraid to ride a bike because I thought if I got my feet tangled in a fall, I could be really hurt. That same month, I was tested for Lupus.

Lupus is a disease that occurs when a body's immune system attacks its own tissues and organs (autoimmune disease). It can be difficult to diagnose because it has signs and symptoms that mimic other ailments. It can be treated but not cured.

Through December 2021, I went through a series of tests and consultations.

In case you haven't been counting, that's four major health setbacks in two years. Can I get back up? God gives us all gifts and he gives us opportunities. He opens the door but he won't make you walk through it. You have to do that on your own.

I can, I did and I will. Stepping up means getting your attitude right.

All In For Family

2021

You might need to make some adjustments, Jeff.

I was born in Boone Memorial Hospital on August 4, 1964. My parents, Nick and Barbara Jarrell, worked hard. They gave my sister Jennifer, my brother Chris and I a good childhood. They worked for the Columbia Gas System and were strong examples of what a positive outlook, a careful plan and lots of love meant.

I attended three elementary schools – Spring Hill, Rock Lake and Richmond – then headed to Spring Hill Junior High School. I graduated from South Charleston High School. I enjoyed baseball. I ran track and cross country. I wanted to play football, but my parents weren't in favor of that. I had a great time my senior year and still managed to keep my grades above average.

I headed to West Virginia State College in the fall after my high school graduation. I had a misconception about college that first year. I thought I was there to run track for the school team and party on the weekends. I ended my freshman year with no real thoughts about a major course of study and a grade point average somewhere between 1 and 2.

I was unaware my path might not be the right one. My parents, however, didn't see it my way. Nick and Barbara handed me my first serious setback.

In a "come to Jesus" talk, they let me know things were going to change. They said they would pay for my books and I would have to pay tuition. At the end of each semester, they'd reimburse me for the tuition *if* I had a grade point average that demonstrated I'd changed my direction and accepted my responsibilities.

I took the warning to heart. I studied harder and improved my grades. I continued to run track. I discovered I could still have fun, as long as I put books before partying. I even held a part-time job at Calculator Sales and Services.

Up to that point, I never had to brush myself off from any big setbacks. I pretty much bounced back up when I faced a challenge and got on with it.

I'm not sure if I thought my own family's story would mimic mine, but I now know from experience that every family is different. Every family has its own rhythms. The ups and downs of family life reflect the people in each family.

A family works when everyone steps up.

Every Child is Different

2003 - Today

Noah has autism.

When our son was a toddler, Joyce began to notice he was quieter than most kids his age. He seemed a bit withdrawn and would be shy in groups. A few visits to the pediatrician and his diagnosis was confirmed. He would need special attention and have challenges. However, he is curious and, once his interest is piqued, he goes all out to learn what he wants to know about. And he wants everyone else to be just as interested as he is.

As a family, we – Joyce, Naomi, Lily and I – accept Noah as he is. We have learned to be patient. We have learned to be understanding. We have learned that he is as productive and important as everyone else in our family.

We step up for Noah.

Because having a family – and being a family – is important to Joyce and me, we have made time to be with our children and encourage them in the things that interest them. We truly believe that every parent opens their hearts to their children, regardless of how they become a family. Once you open your heart, you're in for long haul.

Naomi and Lily were busy girls. They grew up playing sports and involved in activities at school and at church. They learned from their brother that everyone has a place in the world and I am proud of them for that.

Naomi rode horses while she was in grade school. She took art lessons. She loved playing softball. She loves learning. She has a determined sense of what she wants and where she wants to go. It was not a surprise to us that her college search led her to look at schools all along the East Coast.

Lily took dance lessons and was a cheerleader in grade school. She played some basketball in middle school, but fell in love with volleyball and excelled in that sport.

Because our faith is an important part of our lives, we encouraged the girls to participate in programs at our church. Naomi participated in some youth group missions and even traveled to Alaska for one mission. Lily participated in other youth programs.

Noah can be downright dogged about his interests. He is a big sports fan and especially loves Chicago sports. He loves the Cubs and the Bears which we believe come from his lifelong love of animals and watching a favorite television show, "Bear in the Big Blue House."

As each child graduated from high school, we offered to let them decide on a graduation trip. Noah chose to travel to Chicago. And, with his detail-oriented thinking, he planned the trip down to the minute. Since then, he has taken complete responsibility for several guy trips that he and I take together.

Naomi has a penchant for travel. She chose a trip to Amsterdam. She and I had an amazing adventure on our first trip across the ocean.

Lily was ready for fun. Her graduation trip choice was a visit to Florida to go to Disney World and the other family adventure parks there. She chose to bring a friend along. We had a great time.

Because I learned so much from my parents, I knew what it took to be a parent.

Being involved with your children matters. Stepping up for family is important.

Even Though It Hurts

2021

The worst gut punch is the one that seems unfathomable.

On December 20, 2021, Lily moved out of our home. She didn't come home for Christmas and, since then, we have seen her only a few times.

She moved out because we told her to. She had stolen thousands of dollars from us. She'd given most of it away to an Instagram scammer and spent the rest. Even though she was living at home and had a part-time job while she attended West Virginia State University, she told us she was tired of living paycheck to paycheck.

We might not have figured this out as quickly as we did if Joyce had not been going through bank statements. She called me to ask if I knew anything about some deposits Lily had made to her bank account. They were fairly large sums and not the same as her paychecks. Upon investigation, Joyce and I realized the unthinkable: She had taken the money from cash we had in our home. The money, known as "Dad's Stash" was what we used for special expenses and purchases.

How could it happen? Why would she steal from us? Joyce and I were beyond sick over the situation. When we actually realized what was happening, we sat in our living room and cried. We knew we had to confront her. We wanted her to apologize, to offer a reason. We wanted the whole thing to go away.

Lily had no remorse for her decision to take the money. No apologies. No apparent concern about how it affected us or her. Joyce was angry and wanted to know how she thought she could get away with it. I was stunned. I asked her how she could do that when she knew that I had been the victim of a Ponzi scheme myself. She had no reaction.

We decided Lily needed to understand the magnitude of her theft. In a stronger "Come to Jesus" moment like the one I had with my parents so many years ago, I took Lily to the Putnam County Sheriff's office and reported her misdeed. A no-nonsense ex-military man, the sheriff was straightforward with Lily. He told her that she was old enough to be prosecuted as adult and, because of the amount of money, she could get 1 to 5 years in prison.

Though we opted not to prosecute her, the sheriff gave her a warning: If I hear of this again, I will prosecute you myself and no amount of crying from your mommy and daddy will save you.

When Lily and I went to the bank to find out if any of the money could be recovered from the scammer, the bank representative said no. As we left the bank, Lily said, "Why did you have to tell her all of that? You embarrassed me."

This betrayal by our daughter eats at my soul. It breaks my heart. I grieve every day for our loss of Lily. Telling her to move out and dealing publicly with her action has been the hardest thing we've had to do in our marriage. We pray for strength, we play for a positive resolution. Sometimes I pray that it had never happened.

Stand strong. You can't ignore the wrongdoing. You can pray for reconciliation.

Our Paths are Paved With Steps

Today + the Future

Life goes on.

People want books to have endings. Good or bad, happy or sad, the reader wants to see the story wrapped up with "The End". It can be a bow or a knot.

This book is not one of those. I know, as you must through your own experiences, that we are called on every day to step up. Every day, one of us will have a setback of some kind that we will need to face and handle. Sometimes we see those setbacks coming and other times they surprise us.

Regardless of what it is or when it happens, we cannot wallow in self-pity or whine about misfortune. The longer we wallow, the harder it is to climb out of the hole in which we have found ourselves.

Life will sometimes knock you down. When it does, get up and move forward. Step up.

Thank You

This book has been a dream for the last 2 years. It's been an evolution for nearly the last 40 years.

There are many people I'd like to thank, including my wife, Joyce, for your unwavering love, encouragement and support; to my mother, Barbara, who has been there for the entire journey; my children, Noah, Naomi and Lily, I love you all more than you'll ever know; my siblings, Jennifer and Chris, the best sister and brother a guy could have; to my dear friends, Skip Lineberg and Jim Strawn, who encouraged me to make this dream a reality; to the many friend who's love and encouragement over the years helped continue to "step up"; and to my lord and Savior, Jesus Christ, for loving me and making me the man I am today.

Notes

Notes

Notes

www.ingramcontent.com/pod-product-compliance
Lightning Source LLC
Chambersburg PA
CBHW070857050426
42453CB00012B/2250